GW00501949

THE CHRISTIAN
INSTITUTE

Libertarianism

A Christian critique

PHILIP VANDER ELST

First printed in 2003
Reprinted in 2008, 2015 and 2017

ISBN 978-1-901086-22-5

Published by The Christian Institute

Wilberforce House, 4 Park Road, Gosforth Business Park,
Newcastle upon Tyne, NE12 8DG

The Christian Institute is a Company Limited by Guarantee, registered in England as a charity. Company No. 263 4440, Charity No. 100 4774. A charity registered in Scotland. Charity No. SC039220.

Contents

Introduction

What is the value, function and purpose of liberty? What is its place in the moral order? Should individuals be free to consume hardcore pornography and video-nasties, or is there a case for censorship in these areas? Does the State have the right to levy taxes to alleviate poverty, or are private property rights absolute and all taxation theft? Should the power of government be mobilised more energetically in order to 'do good' and advance the welfare of the people, or should the State be viewed with suspicion and its power limited as much as possible? Can liberty survive in an increasingly secular and amoral society, or should the growth of atheism and moral relativism be welcomed? What, in particular, is meant by 'Libertarianism', and what are its strengths and weaknesses?

The need for intelligent examination of these questions is even greater today than it was in 1995, when I last lectured on this subject, because the threats to the survival of a free and civilised society in Britain are growing in extent and intensity.

At the social level, all the destructive trends we have observed since the cultural revolution of the 1960s are either still with us or getting worse, whether we think of crime in general, violence in schools, football hooliganism, the erosion of the traditional family, the spread of sexually transmitted diseases, increasing dishonesty in the workplace, or the growth of alcoholism and drug addiction. At the same time, and partly in response to this, there has been a huge increase in the regulatory power of the State, which, combined with the revolution in information technology, has greatly enhanced its ability to monitor our activities and interfere with our lives.

At the ideological level, the spread of 'political correctness' is gradually eroding freedom of thought and speech by discouraging legitimate criticism of contemporary ideas and fashions. The most obvious example of this is the change that has taken place in the meaning of 'tolerance'. Instead of signifying, as it used to, a readiness to respect the right of individuals to express opinions or engage in activities of which one *disapproves*, the whole concept has been turned on its head so that 'tolerance' now implies *approval*. As a result, those who dare to criticise homosexuality or non-Western cultures and religions, for example, are increasingly stigmatised as 'intolerant' 'homophobes' and 'racists' whose 'bigotry' and 'hate-speech' ought to be curbed to safeguard 'minority rights' and 'multi-culturalism', concepts which are never properly defined or explained.

Underlying this Orwellian corruption of the old liberal idea of tolerance, is the politically correct but question-begging assumption that all cultures and lifestyles are 'equal', and that it is therefore wrong to make critical or 'judgmental' comparisons between, say, single-parenthood and the traditional family, or Christianity and Islam. But is this moral and cultural relativism really justified? Does history suggest that all religions, ideologies and institutions have been equally beneficial? Is it logical to suggest that conflicting philosophies or belief-systems are equally true? Furthermore, if all 'truth' is subjective and therefore illusory, what is the moral justification for making the politically correct value judgment that it is 'wrong' to be 'judgmental'?

Given this background of intellectual confusion and cultural decay, close analysis of the ideology of Libertarianism can throw valuable light on many contemporary political and social issues.

What is Libertarianism and why is it important?

Libertarianism is an eclectic philosophy and movement which is principally American in origin but now has a significant following in Britain and other parts of the English-speaking world. Although it is made up of different political and philosophical strands, and there is plenty of disagreement among Libertarians over particular issues, its core doctrine encapsulates the following propositions:

(1)   The individual is an end in himself and possesses 'natural rights' stemming from the requirements of his nature as an active and rational being;

(2)   The individual mind is the source of all creativity and the fountainhead of all human progress;

(3)   Liberty is the essential condition of all human progress and achievement;

(4)   The right to personal liberty is absolute so long as its exercise does not infringe the equal rights of others;

(5)   Private property rights are also absolute because the individual has an unlimited right to the product of his labour;

(6)   Free market capitalism is the only economic system compatible with freedom and the individual's 'natural rights';

(7)   The role of the State should be strictly limited to the protection of

life, liberty and property, and to the enforcement of contracts;

(8)   Taxation for any other purpose than the protection of life, liberty and property (i.e. to finance the 'Nightwatchman State'), is theft;

(9)   In the areas of sex, marriage, and the family, there are no moral or cultural absolutes: all forms of sexuality, 'marriage', family structures and 'lifestyles' are equally valid and permissible so long as they result from freedom of choice; and

(10)   Since individuals have an absolute right to do what they like with their lives, bodies, and property as long as they respect the rights of others, there should – in a free society – be no restrictions on the consumption or sale (at least by adults) of drugs, pornography, video-nasties, and other perverse substances and forms of 'entertainment'.

Finally, in addition to a belief in these propositions, there is a marked tendency among most (though not all) Libertarians towards atheism and theophobia. By that, I mean they not only tend to disbelieve in the existence of God; they actually dislike the very *idea* of God. To many Libertarians, the possibility that there is a Creator to whom they owe their existence, and to whom they are ultimately accountable for the use they make of their lives, is extremely unwelcome. It not only poses an unacceptable threat to their sense of personal pride and autonomy, but also offends their moral sensibilities, since they equate reverence for God with the totalitarian worship of power. Hence a note of hostility towards theism and Christianity is often sounded in Libertarian literature.

So much, then, by way of a brief description of the essential elements of Libertarian ideology. What about its history? What are its origins and who are some of its key thinkers and advocates? What, if anything, does it have in common with other political and philosophical movements?

Although the intellectual pedigree of Libertarianism can be traced to particular thinkers over the last few centuries, the modern Libertarian movement is mainly a post-war American phenomenon which began to spread outside the United States at the end of the 1970s. With its modern roots in the anti-socialist and isolationist 'Old Right' of the 1930s, whose thinkers were the fiercest opponents of President Roosevelt's 'New Deal', Libertarianism took off in America in the 1960s, and advanced rapidly in the 1970s and '80s. Today, after thirty years of growth and development, it can boast a substantial number of prominent thinkers, publications, and academic 'think tanks', and there is even a Libertarian political party which has contested every American presidential election since 1972.

Whilst there is no single intellectual 'guru' of the Libertarian movement, two thinkers, both of whom are now dead, have had a disproportionate impact on the growth of Libertarianism and the development of its doctrine.

The first, was the female Russian-born writer and philosopher, Ayn Rand, who emigrated to the United States in the 1920s and died in 1982. She founded a philosophical school called 'Objectivism' and expounded her views in non-fictional books like *The Virtue of Selfishness* and *Capitalism: The Unknown Ideal,* but the secret of her wide influence has lain in her eloquent and emotionally powerful philosophical novels, which virtually every Libertarian has read and which are often the entry-point into the Libertarian movement. Of these philosophical novels, the two most famous ones are *The Fountainhead* (1943) and *Atlas Shrugged* (1957). Sales are numbered in millions and they are regularly reprinted. What is their central message and why are they so popular?

The Fountainhead is the story of a brilliant young American architect, called Howard Roark, who defies conventional opinion by refusing to compromise his moral and aesthetic standards in the pursuit of professional success. As such, it is a celebration of individual integrity, creativity and achievement, and its central message – as the title implies – is that the individual ego is the fountainhead of human progress. *Atlas Shrugged,* by contrast, is a much longer book, with a larger cast of characters, and tells the story of how a group of brilliant inventors, businessmen and intellectuals 'stop the motor of the world' in a future socialist America. They go on strike and so ensure that their creative talents cease to prop up what they consider to be an immoral and oppressive social system. Both books, therefore, incorporate similar themes, though their fullest expression is in *Atlas Shrugged*. In it 'altruism' is portrayed as an ascetic, life-hating philosophy which sacrifices the individual to the collective and glorifies the State. *Atlas Shrugged* also contains a savage attack on religion, giving voice to Ayn Rand's theophobic conviction that belief in God is a form of psychological self-abasement which promotes irrationality, obscurantism and tyranny.

Ayn Rand's novels appeal to that spirit of rugged individualism which has always been a strong and widely admired feature of American culture. Unfortunately, by glorifying personal creativity and freedom in the unbalanced way she does, and by equating the idea of 'service' and helping others with coercion and slavery, her philosophy also gratifies personal pride, selfishness, and materialism, as well as appealing to more generous emotions.

The second key figure in the development of the Libertarian movement has been the late Professor Murray Rothbard, an extremely able free-market economist and scholar, whose corpus of work includes books on history and political philosophy as well as economics. Amongst these, the three most influential have been *America's Great Depression; Man, Economy, and State;* and *For a New Liberty.* Whilst the first is a powerful indictment of State mismanagement and regulation of the monetary system, responsible in Rothbard's eyes for the Great Depression of the 1930s, the second is a detailed philosophical exposition of the case for 'anarcho-capitalism' and the abolition of the State. *For a New Liberty,* on the other hand, is a more popular work aimed at a larger audience, and is in effect, as its subtitle indicates, 'The Libertarian Manifesto'. In it Rothbard not only outlines detailed arguments and policies for dismantling the State, in favour of both personal choice and the free market in every area of life, from the regulation of drugs and sexual behaviour, to education, welfare, law and order, and foreign policy. He also sets out, in uncompromising terms, the moral principle upon which the whole of Libertarianism is based.

"The Libertarian creed," he declares, *"rests upon one central axiom: that no man or group of men may aggress against the person or property of anyone else. This may be called the 'nonaggression axiom'. 'Aggression' is defined as the initiation of the use or threat of physical violence against the person or property of anyone else. Aggression is therefore synonymous with invasion.*

If no man may aggress against another...this at once implies that the libertarian stands foursquare for what are generally known as 'civil liberties': the freedom to speak, publish, assemble, and to engage in such 'victimless crimes' as pornography, sexual deviation and prostitution...since the libertarian also opposes invasion of the rights of private property, this also means that he just as emphatically opposes government interference with property rights or with the free-market economy through controls, regulations, subsidies, or prohibitions."

Although it must again be emphasised that Libertarianism is an eclectic creed, with internal differences of opinion between, for example, anarchists and supporters of the 'Minimum State', most Libertarians are familiar with the writings of Rand and Rothbard and share most of their views.

How relevant, though, is Libertarianism to life in 21st century Britain? Extremely, is the short answer.

At the political level, it has exerted a strong influence on the younger and more intellectual elements within the Conservative Party, whilst the numerous publications of the London-based Libertarian Alliance attract many intelligent readers and political activists. It is, however, the cultural impact of Libertarianism which is most significant today. In a nutshell, it both appeals to and reinforces that dislike of authority which is such a marked feature of contemporary British and Western culture. Whilst its attitude to taxation, government regulation, and the Welfare State, is only shared by a small minority, its agnosticism in the area of 'personal morality' and its indifference or hostility towards Christianity puts it firmly in the cultural mainstream.

What is true in Libertarianism?

What can Christians learn from Libertarianism? How much truth is contained in this ideology? A great deal, is again the short answer.

What is true in Libertarianism are the insights it shares with the great Western classical liberal tradition of the 17th, 18th, and 19th centuries, a tradition which also embraces the post-war American Conservative movement and elements within British Conservatism. Of these insights, the first and most important one is religious.

Individuals, the Bible teaches us, are not only made in the image of God, possessing the gifts of reason, conscience and free will, but are also the objects of God's love. It therefore follows that individuals *are* ends in themselves and have *God-given* rights to 'life, liberty, and the pursuit of happiness' – to quote the famous phrase from the American Declaration of Independence. This in turn means that the individual does *not* belong to the State and that all totalitarian political ideologies and systems are therefore immoral and evil.

Libertarians are not only correct in insisting that we have 'natural rights' which no government ought to be allowed to violate; they are also correct in their insistence on the fact that personal liberty is essential to moral growth. Unless we are free to choose between good and evil, right and wrong, we cannot be held responsible for our actions and we cannot learn from our mistakes and grow into better people. It is also true, from a theological point of view, that we cannot enter into a love-relationship with God if our obedience and worship is coerced. That is precisely why God has given us free will, and with it, the ability to think and discover truth. We are not robots to be ordered about by the Church or the State.

If freedom of conscience is essential to moral and spiritual growth, it is also an essential requirement for the pursuit of knowledge and truth, as Milton argued in defence of the freedom of the press in the 17th century, and John Stuart Mill argued in his famous essay *On Liberty* in 1859. Unless we are free to compare and discuss ideas, and to pursue different avenues of inquiry, we cannot grow in our understanding of life, society, and the world in which we live. This is especially important in religion, politics, and science. The more controversial the issue, the more wide-ranging its implications, the more we need to be free to listen to different points of view and form our own opinions. That is why it is essential that political correctness should not be allowed to reduce the ideological space within which it is permitted to debate homosexuality, Islam, the theory of evolution, or any other contemporary ideological 'hot potato'.

The great traditional arguments in defence of 'civil liberties' are extremely compelling and need to be rediscovered and restated in every generation, but does the same apply to private property rights and economic freedom?

Undoubtedly. In the first place, individuals have a right (though not an absolute one) to the product of their labour, especially if that labour has brought into existence resources or benefits which did not previously exist. Secondly, it does not take a genius to realise that private property rights and the right to a free choice of occupation and employment are essential conditions of productive achievement. Without them, personal thrift, creativity and effort are stillborn, and general poverty results, as has been demonstrated in every age and culture, particularly in 20th century socialist countries. But even more important is the fact that the existence of private property and economic freedom is essential to the maintenance of a free society, since power is then diffused throughout society rather than being concentrated in the State. To quote Trotsky's famous and rueful verdict on Soviet Communism in the 1930s: *"In a society in which the sole employer is the State, opposition means death by slow starvation."*

If the 'positive' case for liberty is a powerful one, the 'negative' case is even more conclusive, and is similarly rooted in the inherent nature of human beings. Not only does liberty give us the 'space' we need for personal growth and fulfilment; it also offers some protection against evil by limiting the extent to which we can harm each other.

Here we hit upon a vital truth which Christians, above all others, ought to appreciate, but have all too often forgotten. It is this: since human nature is inherently flawed and imperfect, as we know from our personal lives and are reminded by every news bulletin, power always has a tendency to corrupt unless it is strictly limited and controlled. Even the most benevolent rulers may turn into tyrants if their good intentions are thwarted or their appetites aroused by the temptations of office. It follows from this, that one of the primary functions of any political system, is to create a framework of checks and balances which will prevent governments from oppressing their own citizens. It also suggests that people must not automatically assume that State intervention or regulation is the best answer to every social problem. Politicians and officials are not inherently more virtuous or intelligent than the rest of us, nor are public sector bodies or collective institutions immune to the temptation to pursue their own selfish interests. These truths, moreover, apply to democracies as well as autocracies, since majorities are as likely to elect dictators and oppress minorities as anyone else. The German Jews discovered this in the 1930s, as have many tribes in post-colonial Africa.

For all these reasons, Libertarians are right to be inherently suspicious of the State, particularly when one examines the record of the State throughout history. As the evidence of centuries demonstrates, in different countries and across different cultures, the chief cause of oppression, poverty, and war, has always been tyrannical government. Again and again, it has been the desire of flawed and fallen human beings for power, prestige and pleasure, which has been the chief motive of ruling elites. Hence the recurring pattern throughout history of armed conflict, civil war, oppressive taxation, corruption, injustice, plunder and persecution. Hence, too, the significant fact that the growth of liberty and humanitarianism has been directly linked to the success of particular societies in curbing the power of the State.

If anyone doubts the truth of this general thesis they should read the seminal work in this field by an American political scientist, Professor R.J. Rummel of the University of Hawaii. According to the detailed and exhaustive statistical studies incorporated in his recent books, *Death by Government* and *Power Kills* (Transaction Publishers), **133 million** people were killed in internal repression by tyrannical governments between 30 B.C. and 1900, compared with over **40 million** deaths in war over the same period. In the 20th century, the age of Communism, Fascism and revolutionary socialism in the Third World, the murderous record of the overmighty State has been even more terrible. Between 1900 and 1987, **170 million** people were killed by their own governments, more than **four times** the total number killed in all the wars of that period.

History not only teaches the lesson that power corrupts and government should be limited; it also teaches that this lesson applies to the Church as much as the State. Whilst the Church acted as 'the conscience of kings' and a check on secular rulers during most of the Middle Ages, it often abused power in its own domain and it did not respect freedom of conscience or allow dissent except within very narrow limits. In the 16th and 17th centuries, after the explosion of the Reformation and the fragmentation of Christendom, some Catholics and some Protestants used the power of the State to persecute each other with great cruelty, a pattern of intolerant behaviour which lasted in many parts of Europe well into the 19th century.

What is wrong with Libertarianism?

There is no doubting, then, the strength of the philosophical, theological and historical arguments for liberty. Everything that is true in modern Libertarianism echoes the writings of the great classical liberal thinkers, such as von Humboldt, John Stuart Mill and Herbert Spencer, in the 19th century, and W.H. Mallock, Wilhelm Roepke and F.A. Hayek, in the 20th. Unfortunately, Libertarianism is also a deeply flawed and lopsided ideology.

Its *first* great failing is that it suffers from an idolatrous tendency to make freedom and personal choice an end in itself, forgetting that freedom is only a means to other ends. Some Libertarians may deny this, but their tendency is to regard an argument as won once it is pointed out that an existing restriction or proposal represents an interference with 'freedom of choice' or the operation of the 'free market'. This suggests the criticism is valid, especially in the areas of sexual ethics and popular culture. The question that must be faced, however, is why should we value liberty? Why should we automatically tolerate the 'drug culture', hardcore pornography, violent films, or loud pop concerts in the countryside? Why should we tolerate teenage sex or refrain from criticising adultery and promiscuity?

If, as the great traditional arguments for liberty insist, freedom is essential to the cultivation of goodness, the pursuit of truth and the release of creativity, it follows that freedom derives its value and significance from its anchorage in an objective moral order. But if this is the case, it also follows that it is legitimate to criticise or restrain liberty if its pursuit in any particular instance damages or endangers other important values. Is there not, after all, a conflict between unlimited freedom of expression and the desirability of preserving a civilised culture?

The *second* great failing of Libertarianism is its illogical and unjustified assumption that the right to personal liberty cannot be restricted in one area without inevitably destroying it in others. Why should legal restrictions on the sale and consumption of hardcore pornography or video-nasties inevitably destroy freedom of thought and speech? Why should acceptance of the State's limited right to tax for certain clearly defined purposes inevitably pave the way for a totalitarian State-controlled economy? Is it not possible to achieve a balance between conflicting but good objectives? Why will the 'Tree of Liberty' be cut down just because some of its twigs and branches have been pruned?

This tendency within Libertarianism to rhetorical exaggeration and ideological rigidity reflects a failure to appreciate that even the best and most clearly thought-out philosophy can never encapsulate and do justice to the full complexity of human life and society. It can only offer rough guidelines on which to base choices and decisions, not a foolproof blueprint which covers every eventuality. Nowhere is this more apparent than in the area of 'personal morality'.

The Libertarian rule that personal liberty should only be limited by the obligation on all individuals to respect the equal rights of others, not only ignores the fact that there are other moral values with which a compromise may need to be struck; it also makes the mistake of thinking that there is an absolutely clear and rigid distinction between actions which only affect ourselves, and actions which affect other people. Hence the Libertarian belief that 'victimless crimes' like 'sexual deviancy' and drug addiction should not be restricted or punished by law. The truth, however, is that most of our actions have some impact on other people.

If, for instance, no proper limits are placed on the sale and consumption of video-nasties, pornography, and hard drugs; and no real attempt is made to control the amount of sex, violence, and bad language allowed in films and on television, what is going to be the likely result? Obviously the creation of a cultural environment inimical to the cultivation of courtesy, self-control, marital faithfulness, and consideration for others. Will that not, in turn, undermine the family and encourage every kind of anti-social and criminal behaviour? Is it just a coincidence that the removal of censorship and the rebellion against traditional values which began in the 1960s has been followed by the harmful social trends mentioned at the beginning of this paper?

It is worth remembering that John Stuart-Mill's famous essay, *On Liberty*, specifically stated that freedom was not an unmixed blessing to be enjoyed by all without limit, but a condition which could only be of real benefit to mature adults. To quote his exact words: "*It is, perhaps, hardly necessary to say that this doctrine* [Liberty] *is meant to apply only to human beings in the maturity of their faculties...Liberty, as a principle, has no application to any state of things anterior to the time when mankind has become capable of being improved by free and equal discussion.*"

Does this suggest that the great liberal thinkers of the past would have approved of today's coarse and licentious culture? They would surely be angered by the way in which their high-minded arguments in defence of personal liberty are constantly misused in order to justify giving free rein to the basest human appetites. What, they would ask, is the connection between free inquiry and voyeurism? How is the pursuit of knowledge and truth assisted by the graphic depiction of sexual intercourse or scenes of torture on our film and television screens? What, they might finally ask, is this increasing exposure to a culture of licentiousness and brutality doing to our souls and the souls of our children?

The answer to the last question is that it is not only the quality of our social life which is threatened by the prevailing climate of permissiveness and amorality; freedom itself is endangered.

In the first place, a society whose members are too absorbed in the pursuit of pleasure to develop high standards of personal behaviour, tends to have little respect for moral and intellectual excellence, especially if its cultural leaders preach the subjectivity of all values and treat all choices of 'lifestyle' as a matter of personal taste like food and clothing. This, in turn, produces a truculent and egalitarian mindset which dislikes hierarchy and authority within social institutions like the family, schools and colleges, and other 'private' and non-governmental bodies. The end result is a social vacuum of growing confusion, division and lawlessness, which is filled by an increasingly intrusive and authoritarian State. The parental smack, so to speak, gives way to the policeman's truncheon.

The second reason why contemporary moral decay threatens liberty has to do with the logic of ideas as well as the psychology of human behaviour. If it is generally believed that individuals have the right to do anything they like in their private lives, because moral values are not absolute but a matter of 'personal choice', rulers and officials can similarly argue that they should be able to do whatever they like with power, if this advances their own interests. Moral relativism, in other words, encourages the pursuit of personal gratification and expediency within the organs of the State, and so paves the way to tyranny. Or to put it another way: if totalitarianism is thought of as 'permissiveness with power', the link between moral laxity and despotism becomes even more obvious.

The potential threat to freedom posed by our currently 'permissive' culture, is becoming all the greater, because the damage caused by moral relativism increases if it reinforces existing tendencies towards self-indulgence and violence. As the evidence of history demonstrates, there is a close psychological connection between unchecked lust and physical cruelty and brutality. In both cases, there is a common lack of self-control and a tendency to treat other human beings as objects. Hence the fact that cruel societies are often sexually self-indulgent ones, as ancient Rome was in the first century. To quote the great psychologist, Jung: "*At a time when a large part of mankind is beginning to discard Christianity, it is worth while to understand clearly why it was originally accepted. It was accepted in order to escape at last from the brutality of antiquity. As soon as we discard it licentiousness returns, as is impressively exemplified by life in our large modern cities...we can hardly realize in this day the whirlwinds of the unchained libido which roared through the ancient Rome of the Caesars.*"

Anyone who doubts the truth of Jung's comments should read that great historical classic, *A History of European Morals* (1911), by W.H. Lecky. It not only documents the immorality and cruelty of pagan antiquity, but is also significant because it is the work of a great classical liberal historian and thinker, who, while believing in God, was not a Christian, but a trenchant rationalist critic of the Church.

If Libertarianism deserves criticism because its unbalanced view of liberty helps to weaken the moral and social bonds which hold a civilised society together, what should be our response to the Libertarian dogma that 'taxation is theft' and that there should be no tax-funded public welfare? An equally critical one, is again the answer, for two reasons.

Firstly, property rights ought not to be absolute. Like personal liberty they derive their justification from an ethical system which, at the same time, provides reasonable grounds for their limitation so as to achieve other equally important moral objectives. This means that taxation is not necessarily theft if it advances moral goals or produces moral benefits which would not otherwise be achieved. Taxation must not be excessive or confiscatory, for obvious moral and economic reasons, but it is nonsense to say in principle that it can never be justified to relieve poverty or safeguard public welfare in other ways.

Secondly, helping others who are in need through no fault of their own is a moral duty. We ought to relieve undeserved suffering and increase the opportunities of the poor to live a fuller and happier life than would otherwise be possible. By doing so we help to create a better society because we increase the number of people who can share in the benefits of freedom and contribute their gifts and talents to the common good.

Not only are Libertarians wrong to object to the principle of publicly-funded welfare services, they are also mistaken in their belief that this principle inevitably opens the door to full-blown collectivism. John Stuart Mill was a passionate opponent of State collectivism but in his *Principles of Political Economy* argued that government could have a role in alleviating poverty and promoting education, so long as it was careful to avoid the suppression of private initiative and the creation of both State monopolies and a culture of welfare dependency. This view is now shared, of course, by most British and American Conservatives, and by modern classical-liberal economists like Milton Friedman.

In a similar fashion, the great 19th century Italian liberal, Mazzini, who devoted his whole life to the cause of personal liberty and national self-determination, was a passionate advocate of altruism and the brotherhood of man while remaining firmly opposed to socialism.

In his eloquent book, *The Duties of Man,* Mazzini denounced selfish individualism but made it equally clear that a State-owned and controlled economy is totally destructive of freedom. He also, interestingly enough, criticised atheism and insisted that we have duties to God as well as each other.

This naturally throws the critical spotlight onto Libertarian atheism and theophobia. Is it really true that religious belief is irrational? Is it really the case that reverence for God is a form of self-abasing power-worship which breeds intolerance and is incompatible with the spirit of liberty?

I certainly used to think so, when I was an atheist, so I can understand the emotions of Libertarian theophobes, but I no longer share them. They are neither justified by philosophical analysis nor by the weight of historical evidence.

To begin with, it is the rationality of atheism, rather than belief in God, which is truly questionable. To accept atheism, you have to believe that our extraordinary universe, with all its amazingly complex life-forms, structures, and scientific laws, is simply the accidental consequence of random physical and chemical processes. Is this really credible? Is it likely that whereas computers are the deliberately designed products of human intelligence, the infinitely more complex human brains which created them are the unintended by-products of the accidental collision of atoms? If there were only one improbability to account for in our universe, atheism would not seem so ridiculous, but there are thousands of them! Think of the immune system in our bodies, or the chemical factory of the human liver, or the migratory and nest-building instincts of birds, or the amazing structure and operation of the genetic code. Is it credible that the existence of these structures and processes is purely accidental? Is it not as absurd to believe this as it would be to believe that the Oxford English Dictionary was produced by an explosion in a printing works?

Atheists commonly argue that evolutionary theory can explain the world without introducing the idea of God, but this too is nonsense, even if one ignores the growing scientific critique of evolution. As various mathematicians have pointed out, the statistical odds against the accidental emergence of complex organisms are not lessened by the suggestion that their development has taken place only very gradually over a long period. A sequence of a hundred improbable steps, however small, is just as unlikely as the emergence of a complex organ or function in one random leap. In any case, all this misses the point. The real intellectual challenge facing atheists is not to explain how life in all its complexity came into being by accident; it is to explain why this is *more* probable than the opposite hypothesis, that intelligent life has an intelligent supernatural cause in the form of a Divine Creator.

Libertarian atheists are confronted by an even greater problem nearer home. They cannot explain human consciousness, and therefore their own capacity to think, choose, and discover moral values, including the desirability of liberty.

If atheism is true, our minds are wholly dependent on our brains (we have no souls) and our brains are an accidental by-product of the physical universe. But if this is the case, it means that all our thoughts, beliefs, and choices, are simply the inevitable end result of a long chain of non-rational causes. How then can we have free will or attach any validity or importance to our reasoning processes? If we are bound to think or behave the way we do because of our internal biochemistry, how can we be free agents or know that we are in possession of objective truths about science, ethics, or politics? If our perception and use of the rules of logic are merely the inevitable end product of a long chain of random and non-rational physical and chemical events, how can we know that our examination of facts and arguments yields real knowledge? Surely, if atheism is true, our thoughts and values have no more significance than the sound of the wind in the trees, as C.S. Lewis argued in his book, *Miracles* (Fontana-Collins), and E.L. Mascall demonstrated in his 1956 Bampton Lectures, *Christian Theology and Natural Science.*

The truth, however, is that we *can* think and reason validly, since to argue that we *can't,* itself involves an act of reasoning and is therefore self-contradictory. We cannot 'know' that we know nothing! Our belief that we have free will is similarly valid, not only because we are aware of our capacity to choose between alternatives and change our minds, but because the denial of free will *also* involves the use of a self-contradictory argument. If all our reasoning is solely 'determined' by our physical constitution and is therefore not 'free', so too is the belief that we have no free will, so how can we know it is true? It is an argument that refutes itself.

But if logical reasoning tells us that we genuinely possess free will and the capacity to think and discover truth, how do we explain this? Surely the best and only answer is that we are spiritual as well as material beings, and as such, are the creation of an eternal, self-existent intelligence outside ourselves and the physical universe, whom we call God.

Our awareness of objective moral norms and values has similarly theistic implications. We cannot explain away our innate sense of right and wrong by saying that our moral perceptions are instincts, since our instincts are often in conflict with each other, and are themselves in need of moral adjudication before we can know how we ought to act. Our feeling that we ought to repress our survival instinct in order to follow our instinct to help a drowning stranger who has fallen into a freezing lake, for example, results from our awareness of a moral obligation to save life and relieve suffering. The question is, however, from where does this sense of moral obligation come? It is obviously not an expression of our desires and emotions, since our moral sense is often in conflict with them. We want to commit adultery with beautiful women but we know we ought not to break our marriage vows. We get angry with a person who challenges our political views, but we control our tempers because we know we ought to respect the freedom of thought and speech of others. Can our moral sense perhaps be justified or explained on utilitarian grounds? After all, we know that theft and murder is wrong because it is bad for society. But why should we care about the good of society? Why should we care about the rights and interests of other people if, because of our strength and cleverness, we can have a more enjoyable life by ignoring them?

In the end, unless we are moral nihilists, we must recognise that our moral perceptions about the value of life and liberty, and the rules we must obey in order to safeguard society, are self-evident truths, or axioms. As such, they are as rational and objective as the rules of logic and mathematics, and failure to understand them is the moral equivalent of colour-blindness. But if *this* is the case, how can it be explained or justified if human beings are only biological machines put together by chance in an accidental universe? How can their moral 'thoughts' have any inherent meaning or significance? Only, surely, if the Moral Law 'written on our hearts' is somehow a reflection of an eternal, self-existent 'Goodness' outside ourselves and 'behind' or 'beyond' the physical order of 'Nature', in other words, God.

Libertarian atheism, then, cuts its own throat philosophically and, by doing so, deprives liberty of any firm philosophical foundation. Belief in the existence and goodness of God is far more rational than disbelief. Even the problem of evil does not really shift the balance of the debate, since it cannot be used as an argument against God's existence if the moral standard by which we judge reality is purely subjective. If, on the other hand, our moral standard is not subjective but true and absolute, its very existence cannot be explained without reference to God, and the problem of evil therefore requires a better explanation than atheism.

Why Libertarian theophobia is misguided

Libertarian theophobia is not only foolish because atheism is philosophically untenable; it is also misguided because it ignores the obvious implications of the discovery of God's existence and nature.

If reason, let alone revelation, tells us that we are the products of an infinitely good, loving, and powerful Creator, it means that we owe the gift of life to God. It means that our whole being, our whole capacity to think, and feel, and act, is dependent on God, who not only created all that exists, but sustains it in being. How, then, can we regard Him, or the very idea of Him, as tyrannical? How can we argue against God when He alone enables us to think and reason, and is the source of all our moral perceptions? How, given who God is, can He ever be in the wrong and we, somehow, in the right? The whole notion is surely absurd and pathetically presumptuous and arrogant.

The truth is, if God is our Creator, to knowingly ignore or reject Him is to be like a plant that refuses to grow towards the sunlight. It is an act of ingratitude and supreme idiocy. If, on top of this, we subsequently reject His grace and forgiveness, it will separate us in eternity from the true source of all life, love, and joy.

What, then, is the proper response to God, and how should this affect the way we think about liberty?

As the Bible repeatedly teaches us, our first and most important duty is to love, honour, and obey our Creator, who has made us in His image, and has given us free will, so that we can share His love, His life, and His joy. Reason and the Bible also tell us that all our gifts, talents, and resources, come from God and are therefore to be used in His service to make the world a better place to live in. This means that God gives us the wonderful opportunity to share in His continuous creative act, by making our own personal contribution to the pursuit of beauty, knowledge, and goodness. Since we are not biological robots, but have free will, we can either make good use of our freedom or prey on other lives and become evil. If we make the wrong choice, we cannot blame God for the suffering we inflict on ourselves and others.

Our knowledge of the Moral Law not only reveals our link with God and challenges us to love and obey Him; it is also an essential part of our inner freedom to choose and act. Without this sense of right and wrong, our ability to control our desires and appetites, and resist our worst impulses, gradually weakens, and we eventually lose control over our wills and actions.

If it is the case that a belief in objective moral values sustains our inner freedom and teaches us our duties towards each other, what is likely to happen if people stop believing in God? The answer ought to be obvious. Belief in the absoluteness of the Moral Law will tend to wither, and the fear of violating it will also tend to vanish, since it is no longer perceived to have an eternal sanction behind it. This in turn will sooner or later have a predictably harmful effect on personal behaviour.

That is precisely what has happened in our increasingly godless and secularised Western societies. As high-minded 19th century agnostics like T.H. Huxley and George Eliot feared, not to mention Matthew Arnold and Dostoyevsky, the erosion of religious belief and Christianity in the West has been followed, after a long time-lag, by the cultural and social decay we see around us today. As a result, liberty itself is now in danger of committing suicide, because the moral self-discipline required to sustain a free and civilised society is rapidly disappearing.

Libertarian theophobia not only encourages licence and social dissolution: it also fails to see the importance of the State in restraining evil in society – something St Paul refers to in Romans 13. The greater the lack of moral self-discipline in society, the more the State will be forced to intrude in personal affairs. As the great Conservative philosopher, Edmund Burke, famously observed in the 18th century: "Society cannot exist unless a controlling power on will and appetite be placed somewhere, and the less of it there is within, the more there must be without."

Our modern day cultural and social decay would not have surprised the great philosophers and statesmen of the old Western liberal tradition. As an American scholar, M. Stanton Evans, has shown in his book, *The Theme Is Freedom: Religion, Politics, And The American Tradition,* (Regnery, 1994), most of these figures were Christians, from Aquinas and John of Salisbury in the Middle Ages, to Milton, Sidney, and Locke in the 17th century, and the 'Founding Fathers' of the United States in the 18th century. It is therefore appropriate that I should conclude with George Washington's famous warning to his countrymen, contained in his farewell address to Congress as America's first President (17 September 1796):

"Of all the dispositions and habits which lead to political prosperity, religion and morality are indispensable supports...Let it simply be asked where is the security for property, for reputation, for life, if the sense of religious obligation deserts the oaths which are the instruments of investigation in Courts of Justice? And let us with caution indulge the supposition that morality can be maintained

without religion. Whatever may be conceded to the influence of refined education on minds of peculiar structure, reason and experience both forbid us to expect that national morality can prevail in exclusion of religious principle."